States CONNECTICUT

by Jason Kirchner

CAPSTONE PRESS
a capstone imprint

Next Page Books are published by Capstone Press,
1710 Roe Crest Drive, North Mankato, Minnesota 56003
www.mycapstone.com

Library of Congress Cataloging-in-Publication Data
Cataloging-in-publication information is on file with the Library of
Congress.
ISBN 978-1-5157-0393-8 (library binding)
ISBN 978-1-5157-0453-9 (paperback)
ISBN 978-1-5157-0505-5 (ebook PDF)

Editorial Credits
Jaclyn Jaycox, editor; Kazuko Collins and Katy LaVigne, designer;
Morgan Walters, media researcher; Laura Manthe, production specialist

Photo Credits
Alamy: North Wind Picture Archives, 26, RosaIreneBetancourt 3, 11;
Capstone Press: Angi Gahler, map 4, 7; Corbis: Burstein Collection, top
left 20; CriaImages.com: Jay Robert Nash Collection, top right 21, top
18; Dreamstime: Americanspirit, middle 18; iStockphoto: traveler1116,
bottom 19; Library of Congress: Prints and Photographs Division
bottom 18, top 19; North Wind Picture Archives: 25, 27; One Mile
Up, Inc., flag, seal 22-23; Shutterstock: barbsimages, bottom right 8,
barbsimages, 16, Bildagentur Zoonar GmbH, bottom right 20, BluIz60,
top left 21, Chris Hill, bottom left 20, Christopher Halloran, middle 19,
cvrestan, 10, Everett Historical, 12, 28, f11photo, 9, Filatova Liubov, top
24, Jeff Schultes, 15, kaband, middle right 21, Kentaro Foto, bottom
24, Matteo Chinellato, bottom right 21, Melinda Fawver, top right
20, Michael Richardson, 7, Nancy Kennedy, cover, Richard Cavalleri,
6, Ritu Manoj Jethani, 17, Romiana Lee, bottom left 8, Sean Pavone,
5, 13, Shane Gross, middle left 21; Wikimedia: Office of History and
Preservation, U.S. House of Representatives, 29, Smokeybjb, bottom left
21, Sphilbrick, 14

All design elements by Shutterstock

Printed and bound in China.
0316/CA21600187
012016   009436F16

TABLE OF CONTENTS

Want to take your research further? Ask your librarian if your school subscribes to PebbleGo Next. If so, when you see this helpful symbol (➤) throughout the book, log onto www.pebblegonext.com for bonus downloads and information.

LOCATION

Connecticut is a very small state in the far northeastern corner of the country. North of Connecticut is Massachusetts. To the west is New York. Rhode Island lies to its east. Connecticut's southern coast faces Long Island Sound, which is an arm of the Atlantic Ocean. Hartford, the state's capital, lies along the Connecticut River in the center of the state. Bridgeport, New Haven, Hartford, and Stamford are the state's biggest cities.

PebbleGo Next Bonus!
To print and label your own map, go to www.pebblegonext.com and search keywords:

CT MAP

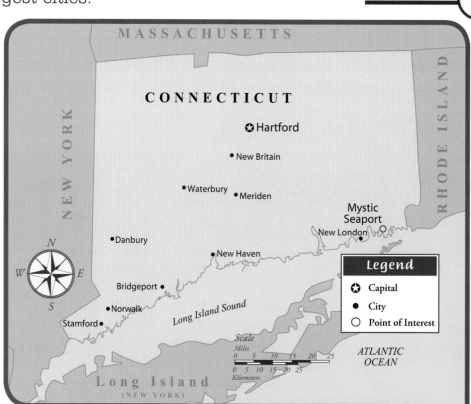

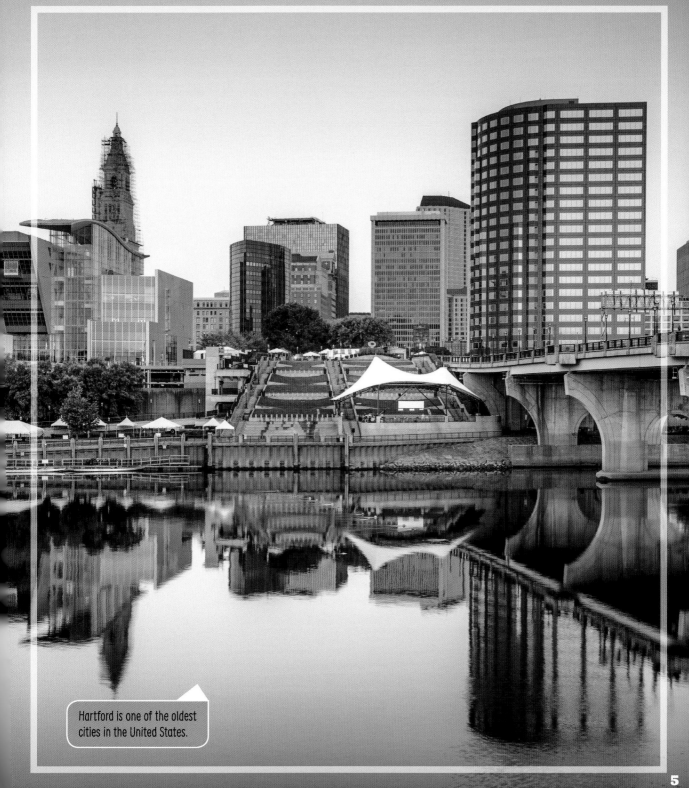

Hartford is one of the oldest
cities in the United States.

GEOGRAPHY

Connecticut's land has four regions. The Eastern and Western Uplands sit on both sides, with the flatter Central Lowland between them. The best farmland is in the Central Lowland. The narrow Coastal Lowland runs along the southern border of Connecticut. Beaches, bays, marshes, and rocky shores line Connecticut's coast. The Connecticut River flows through the center of the state. Connecticut's highest point is in the Western Upland. Mount Frissell stands 2,380 feet (725 meters) above sea level. It is in the northwest corner of Connecticut.

The Housatonic River is 149 miles (240 kilometers) long and flows through western Connecticut.

Scale
Miles
0 5 10 15 20 25
0 5 10 15 20 25
Kilometers

Mount Frissell

EASTERN UPLAND

N
W   E
S

CENTRAL LOWLAND

Naugatuck River

Housatonic River

Connecticut River

Thames River

Lake Candlewood

WESTERN UPLAND

COASTAL LOWLAND

ATLANTIC OCEAN

Long Island Sound

Legend
▲ Highest Point
⬭ Lake
〰 River

Rocky Neck State Park covers 710 acres (287 hectares) and various terrains in the town of East Lyme.

WEATHER

Winters and summers in Connecticut are mild, but the temperature can quickly change. The average summer temperature is 69 degrees Fahrenheit (21 degrees Celsius). The average winter temperature is 28°F (-2°C).

Average High and Low Temperatures (Bridgeport, CT)

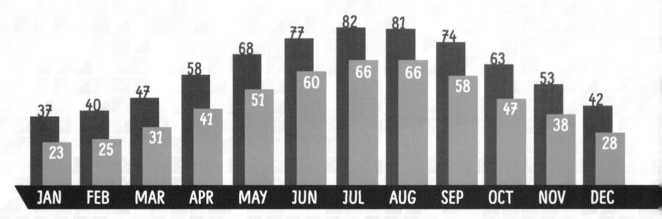

Month	High	Low
JAN	37	23
FEB	40	25
MAR	47	31
APR	58	41
MAY	68	51
JUN	77	60
JUL	82	66
AUG	81	66
SEP	74	58
OCT	63	47
NOV	53	38
DEC	42	28

LANDMARKS

Mark Twain House and Museum

Author Mark Twain wrote *The Adventures of Tom Sawyer* and other popular books. He lived in Connecticut for many years. His Victorian home in Hartford is a state monument. Many tourists visit every year. They see the same furniture he used every day.

PebbleGo Next Bonus!
To watch a video about
Mystic Seaport, go to
www.pebblegonext.com
and search keywords:

CT VIDEO

Mystic Seaport

Mystic Seaport in southeastern Connecticut was designed to look like a whaling village from the 1800s. Visitors see where sails, ropes, and other sailing gear were made. The schoolhouse has old desks, a woodstove, and a blackboard. A famous pizza parlor is also in Mystic. The 1988 movie *Mystic Pizza* made the town famous.

Mashantucket Pequot Museum

The Mashantucket Pequot Museum in southeastern Connecticut brings the Indian nation to life. The museum offers films, lifelike exhibits, and artifacts to show what life was like for these American Indians. The highlight is a life-size Pequot village of the 1500s. Visitors learn how the Pequot built wigwams and made arrows.

HISTORY AND GOVERNMENT

The British Redcoats retreat during the 1775 Revolutionary War battle at Concord.

Before Europeans arrived, Algonquian Indians lived in Connecticut. The Pequot people were the major tribe of the Algonquian. In the 1600s Great Britain began setting up colonies. In 1633 colonists founded Windsor. This was Connecticut's first permanent European settlement. Soon other colonists built Wethersfield and Hartford. These three towns became the Connecticut Colony in 1636. Britain's King Charles II made Connecticut a British colony in 1662. Connecticut soldiers joined the other American colonists in the Revolutionary War (1775–1783). The colonists won their freedom from Great Britain in 1783. In 1788 Connecticut became the 5th U.S. state.

Connecticut's state government has three branches. The governor leads the executive branch, which carries out laws. The legislature is made up of the 36-member Senate and the 151-member House of Representatives. Judges and their courts make up the judicial branch. They uphold the laws.

Connecticut's state capitol building is located in Hartford.

INDUSTRY

Manufacturing has always been important to Connecticut's economy. Connecticut was an early manufacturing center. Today, factories in Connecticut make rocket motors, space suits, submarines, airplane engines, and small boats. Connecticut also makes chemical products, electrical equipment, and machine tools.

Service industries are a large part of Connecticut's economy. Insurance, moneylending, and real estate are the top services. The U.S. insurance industry began in Hartford. Today more than 100 insurance companies have their headquarters in Connecticut.

Connecticut General Life Insurance Company is one of the oldest in the state. Its headquarters is located in Bloomfield.

About 10 percent of Connecticut's land is farmland. Agriculture is a small but important part of its economy. Shade tobacco is one of the largest crops. The state also produces eggs, milk, and beef cattle.

Connecticut shade tobacco is grown under large tents that protect the leaves from the sun.

POPULATION

Almost all of Connecticut's first immigrants were from England. Many more immigrants arrived in the late 1800s and early 1900s. These people came from Ireland, Italy, Germany, Russia, and many other nations. Many of their descendants still live in Connecticut. Most of Connecticut's population is white. More than 2.5 million white people live in the state. Large populations of African-Americans and Hispanics live in Hartford, New Haven, and Bridgeport. Nearly one-half million people in Connecticut are Hispanic. Small populations of Asians and American Indians also live in Connecticut.

Population by Ethnicity

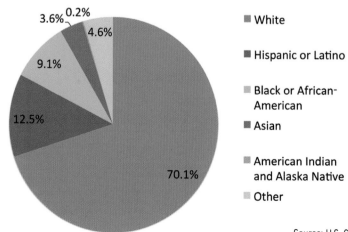

- 3.6%
- 0.2%
- 4.6%
- 9.1%
- 12.5%
- 70.1%

■ White

■ Hispanic or Latino

■ Black or African-American

■ Asian

■ American Indian and Alaska Native

■ Other

Source: U.S. Census Bureau.

The annual UBS Parade Spectacular in Stamford draws over 100,000 people.

BUS STOP
CT TRANSIT
203·327·7433
Routes:
13·31·32
33·34
41·42·45

PARADE
ROUT

FAMOUS PEOPLE

Mark Twain (1835–1910) is one of America's best-loved authors. He wrote *The Adventures of Tom Sawyer* while living in Hartford. He was born in Missouri as Samuel Clemens.

Ralph Nader (1934–) is an activist for consumers' rights. He has fought for safe cars, safe food, and many other causes. He's also been a presidential candidate five times. He was born in Winsted.

Harriet Beecher Stowe (1811–1896) worked to outlaw slavery. Stowe wrote the antislavery novel *Uncle Tom's Cabin*. She was born in Litchfield.

Eli Whitney (1765–1825) invented the cotton gin. It separates the cotton seeds from the fibers. His factories for cotton gins and guns called muskets were in New Haven. He was born in Massachusetts.

George W. Bush (1946–) was the 43rd president of the United States (2001–2009). He served as the governor of Texas from 1995 to 2000. He was born in New Haven.

Noah Webster (1758–1843) compiled *An American Dictionary of the English Language* in 1828. It has been revised many times. He was born in West Hartford.

STATE SYMBOLS

Tree

Charter oak

Flower

mountain laurel

Bird

American robin

Insect

European mantis

PebbleGo Next Bonus! For a recipe using a popular Connecticut spice, go to www.pebblegonext.com and search keywords:
CT RECIPE

Folk Dance

square dance

Ship

USS *Nautilus*

Animal

sperm whale

Shellfish

eastern oyster

Fossil

Eubrontes giganteus

Mineral

garnet

FAST FACTS

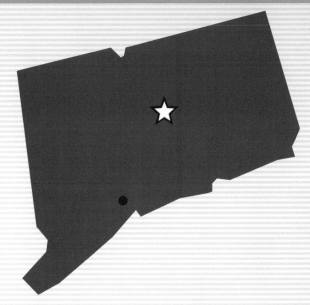

STATEHOOD
1788

CAPITAL ☆
Hartford

LARGEST CITY •
Bridgeport

SIZE
4,842 square miles (12,541 square kilometers) land area
(2010 U.S. Census Bureau)

POPULATION
3,596,080 (2013 U.S. Census estimate)

STATE NICKNAME
Constitution State, Nutmeg State

STATE MOTTO
"Qui Transtulit Sustinet," which is Latin for "He who
transplanted still sustains"

STATE SEAL

Connecticut's original state seal was created in 1639. It showed a field of grapevines and the state motto that the flag bears. Over time the number of grapevines has been reduced to just three. The words "Sigillum Reipublicae Connecticutensis" were added around 1784. They are Latin for "Seal of the State of Connecticut."

PebbleGo Next Bonus!
To print and color your own flag, go to www.pebblegonext.com and search keywords:

CT FLAG

STATE FLAG

Connecticut's state flag was adopted in 1897. It features a white shield on a blue background. The shield is bordered in gold and silver. Three grapevines are in the center. The grapevines stand for Connecticut's early colonists. Like transplanted vines, they "transplanted" themselves to their new home. Below them is a banner with the state motto, "Qui Transtulit Sustinet." It is Latin for "He who transplanted still sustains."

MINING PRODUCTS
traprock, sand and gravel

MANUFACTURED GOODS
transportation equipment, chemicals, fabricated metal products, electrical equipment, computers and electronic equipment, machinery, food products

FARM PRODUCTS
home and garden plants, milk, chickens, eggs, tobacco

PROFESSIONAL SPORTS TEAMS
New England Seawolves (AFL)

PebbleGo Next Bonus!
To learn the lyrics to
the state song, go to
www.pebblegonext.com
and search keywords:
CT SONG

CONNECTICUT TIMELINE

1614
Dutch explorer Adriaen Block sails up the Connecticut River and maps the region. He claims Connecticut for the Dutch.

1620
The Pilgrims establish a colony in the New World in present-day Massachusetts.

1633
Colonists found Windsor in north-central Connecticut. It is Connecticut's first English settlement.

1636
Hartford, Wethersfield, and Windsor settlers form the Connecticut Colony.

1637
The Pequot War is fought between colonists and the Pequot Indians. Colonists attack a Pequot fort at Mystic in southeastern Connecticut. Hundreds of Pequot people are killed. The Pequots are forced to leave the area in 1638.

1638

A group of planters found the New Haven colony in southern Connecticut. They buy the land from the Quinnipiac Indians.

1662

King Charles II gives the Connecticut Colony a royal document called a charter. The charter gives the Connecticut colonists more independence from England.

1775–1783

American colonists fight for independence from the British in the Revolutionary War. More than 3,000 men from Connecticut join the battle. Connecticut provides weapons and supplies to the American soldiers.

1788

Connecticut becomes the 5th state on January 9.

1810 The first insurance company is founded in Hartford. The company is the ancestor of today's ITT Hartford Group.

1833 Teacher Prudence Crandall opens New England's first academy for African-American women in Canterbury in eastern Connecticut.

1861–1865 The Union and the Confederacy fight the Civil War. Connecticut fights for the Union. More than 50,000 Connecticut men fight in the war.

1914–1918 World War I is fought; the United States enters the war in 1917.

1938 The Great Hurricane hits the East Coast, including Connecticut. The hurricane brings damaging winds and flooding. Many homes, businesses, and boats are destroyed. Hundreds of people die in the storm.

1939–1945 World War II is fought; the United States enters the war in 1941.

1954 The first nuclear submarine is invented and launched in Groton in southeastern Connecticut.

1955 In August hurricanes Connie and Diane hit Connecticut one week apart. Floods caused by the hurricanes kill 77 people, hurt 4,700 others, and cause more than $350 million in damage. Floodwaters wash away downtown Winsted in northwestern Connecticut.

1974 Ella Grasso is elected governor of Connecticut. She is the state's first female governor.

1982 The first artificial heart is invented by Dr. Robert Jarvik of Stamford.

2014 The University of Connecticut's men's and women's basketball teams, the Connecticut Huskies, win national titles.

2015 Connecticut becomes the first state to end chronic homelessness among veterans.

Glossary

artificial *(ar-tuh-FI-shuhl)*—made by people

chemical *(KE-muh-kuhl)*—a substance used in or produced by chemistry; medicines, gunpowder, and food preservatives are all made from chemicals

descendant *(di-SEN-duhnt)*—your descendants are your children, their children, and so on into the future

equipment *(i-KWIP-muhnt)*—the machines and tools needed for a job or an activity

executive *(ig-ZE-kyuh-tiv)*—the branch of government that makes sure laws are followed

immigrant *(IM-uh-gruhnt)*—someone who comes from one country to live permanently in another country

industry *(IN-duh-stree)*—a business which produces a product or provides a service

legislature *(LEJ-iss-lay-chur)*—a group of elected officials who have the power to make or change laws for a country or state

marsh *(MARSH)*—an area of wet, low land

nuclear *(NOO-klee-ur)*—having to do with the energy created by splitting atoms; nuclear reactors on subs use this energy as a power source

region *(REE-juhn)*—a large area

Read More

Boehme, Gerry. *Connecticut.* It's My State! New York: Cavendish Square Publishing, 2015.

Ganeri, Anita. *United States of America: A Benjamin Blog and His Inquisitive Dog Guide.* Country Guides. Chicago: Heinemann Raintree, 2015.

Rissman, Rebecca. *What's Great About Connecticut?* Our Great States. Minneapolis: Lerner Publications, 2015.

Internet Sites

FactHound offers a safe, fun way to find Internet sites related to this book. All of the sites on FactHound have been researched by our staff.

Here's all you do:

Visit *www.facthound.com*

Type in this code: 9781515703938

Super-cool stuff! Check out projects, games and lots more at **www.capstonekids.com**

Critical Thinking Using the Common Core

1. How much of Connecticut's land is farmland? What do they grow? (Key Ideas and Details)

2. The small state of Connecticut is made up of four different land regions. What are they? (Key Ideas and Details)

3. Many descendants of the first people to live in Connecticut still live there today. What is a descendant? (Craft and Structure)

Index